GARY JONES

Charleston Travel Guide

This book was professionally typeset on Reedsy.
Find out more at reedsy.com

Contents

Introduction

I want to thank you and congratulate you for downloading the book, "Charleston Travel Guide: How to Make The Most Out of Your 3-Day Charleston Vacation".

Charleston is no California or New York. It is a big city with a small town vibe. It has an unparalleled Southern hospitality that makes you feel at home. It has breathtaking sceneries and an interesting skyline. Charleston is a little bit of everything. It has stunning beach towns. It has thriving business districts and streets filled with colorful antebellum buildings. It also has a number of towering churches. It's no wonder that it's called the Holy City.

There's a lot to see and do in Charleston. You can visit one of its beach towns. You can surf or walk on a historic street. You could see old trees or go to its fantastic museums.

This book is your ultimate Charleston travel guide. In this book, you'll learn:

- The interesting history of Charleston
- The reasons why you should visit the "holy city"
- What's the best time to visit this city
- The best landmarks and tourist spots in Charleston

- The best budget hotels in the city
- The unique things to do in Charleston
- The best bars and night clubs
- The best restaurants and cafes
- Historical houses that you should see
- The Charleston weather
- Neighborhoods, shopping streets, and islands to explore
- And more!

Charleston College

This book contains insider tips that will have you save money and get the best out of your Charleston vacation.

Charleston is one of the most beautiful cities you'll ever see. Its streets are lined with colorful old buildings, churches, and lovely palmetto trees. There's also something about its cobblestone roads that make you feel like you're strolling in another time or world.

The holy city exudes warmth, beauty, and serenity. It's also a bit transformative. There's something about this city that makes you want to make positive changes in your life. The scenic views calms your soul and the historic houses make you think about America's fascinating past.

If you ever feel like you want to recharge and get stress out of your system, head to the holy city. A short visit to Charleston is powerful enough to nourish your soul.

Thank you again for downloading this book and I hope that you enjoy it!

1

All About Chucktown

Charleston, South Carolina (or Chucktown) is hailed as one of the friendliest and safest cities in the world. It is slowly becoming one of the top resort cities in the United States. It's nestled on the Atlantic coast. The city's coastline is strategically positioned in between the coastlines of Miami and Washington, D. C. There's something about this city that makes you want to fall in love. It's filled with historical landmarks, breathtaking sites, fascinating colors, stunning beaches, and interesting flavors.

What makes Charleston special is that it's a little bit of something. It's a modern city with an old town vibe. It also has beautiful beaches. It has the right combination of the culture, the arts, great food, shopping sites, and the sea. It's definitely a stunning paradise. It is one of the most picturesque cities in the United States.

The city exudes the warmth associated with the Southern hospitality. You could see warm smiles and friendly people anywhere you look. The people living in Charleston are hospitable, warm, and welcoming.

Charleston has stunning churches and colorful buildings. It is definitely a laid back southern paradise. It has long beach lines and five lovely beach towns. The whole city is picture-perfect. It almost looks like an oasis. It also has a number of surf breaks, making it a surfer's nirvana.

Charleston is one of the oldest English Colonies in America. So, it's no surprise that you'll find splendid rainbow colored Georgian buildings around the city.

But, Charleston is not all butterflies, colors, and sunshine. It has its share of tragedies. It has gone through wars, fires, earthquakes, Yankee bombardments, and hurricanes. But, like its people, Charleston is resilient. After every challenge, the city becomes better, stronger, and more beautiful.

The Holy City

Charleston is considered as the Holy City because of its tolerance of all religions. This city is considered the home of immigrants from England, Scotland, Germany, France, and Ireland. These immigrants brought various religious, such as Roman Catholic, Judaism, and various types of Protestantism.

Charleston is also known as the "holy city" because it's the home of many historic and towering churches, including the St. Michael's Church, St. Philip's Church, the Second Presbyterian Church, and the St. Mary's Catholic Church. It is also the home of various Lutheran, Baptist, Methodist, Orthodox, Catholic, Episcopal, Presbyterian, and United Pentecoastal churches. It also has two Jewish Synagogues.

This holy city of the south is no Vatican. But, there's something about this city that's relaxing and blissful. It almost feels like heaven on Earth.

The Fascinating History of Charleston, South Carolina

Charleston is the third largest city in South Carolina and it is the capital of Charleston County. It was once the wealthiest city in the South and it's still considered as one of the one of the longest, most historic, and most diverse communities in the United States.

In 1660, Charles II was restored to the throne with the help of his loyal friends known as the "Lord Proprietors". To express his gratitude, he granted the Lords the title to the Chartered Province of Carolina in 1663. It took the Lords seven years to prepare and arrange for their settlement expeditions. In 1670, Governor William Sayle traveled to Carolina with hundreds of Settlers from Bermuda. These colonists settled on the bank of the Ashley River. At that time, the area was still occupied by Cusabo Indians. But, in 1671, the colonists waged war against them. After losing the war, the Cusabo Indians fled the area and those left were turned into slaves.

The Charlestown settlement soon grew following the arrival of settlers from Virginia, Barbados, and England. They called this place "Charles Town" in honor of King Charles II. This town continued to grow and was later called Charleston.

Charleston was used as a colonial seaport during its early days. But, it later grew to become one of the wealthiest cities in the United States. The city exports cotton and rice. It was the home of wealthy entrepreneurs, industrialists, and landowners.

On April 1861, the Confederate states (slave states) soldiers fired on the union- occupied Fort Sumter located in the Charleston Harbor. This is the beginning of the Civil War. Charleston suffered the consequences of the war for a very long time. The city slowly repaired and rebuilt a few of its historically significant architectural gems. The rice and cotton fields were destroyed. A lot of merchants abandoned agriculture and resorted to trade and industry.

In 1904, a navy yard was constructed in Charleston. This strengthened the city's economy. Factories are built and the city's port activities have significantly increased after the civil war. The tourism and the medical industry also flourished.

Today, Charleston is still one of the wealthiest cities in the United States. Because of its well-preserve architectural gems and beautiful beaches, this city has also become one of the most thriving tourist spots in the country. It was hailed as the America's most friendly city in 2011, 2013, and 2014. It was also considered as the most hospitable and polite city in the United States. In 2016, Travel + Pleasure hailed Charleston as the best city in the world.

2

The Most Famous Landmarks in the City

Charleston is more than just a seaport city and agricultural paradise. It is also slowly becoming one of the most popular tourist spots in the United States, thanks to its picturesque views, colorful buildings, and historical landmarks. Below are the most popular landmarks in America's holy city.

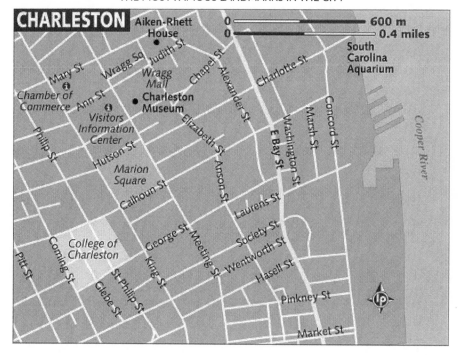

The Battery

The Battery is one of the most popular landmarks in the city. It is a defensive promenade and a seawall. It's located on the southernmost part of the Charleston peninsula. It's a scenic place where the Ashley River and Copper River meet.

The Battery

The Battery gives you a scenic view of the Charleston harbor. It also has a picturesque waterfront park where you could find the famous pineapple fountain.

The East Battery Street is lined with palm trees and beautiful colonial antebellum houses.

It almost feels like you're in a different country. It is the home of pastel-colored colonial mansions. This place is so beautiful that you won't believe that this was, in fact, a coastal defense artillery battery during the civil war.

There's a lot to see in the Battery. You can take a horse carriage ride around the area. You can take a photo next to the pineapple fountain, or you could see more Southern-Style mansions on Battery Street. You could also walk along a path lined with oyster shells.

You can also stroll in the White Point Garden Park, amidst the haunting and stunning oak trees. You can see two cannons (columbiads) used during the civil war and a few military monuments, including the Sergeant Jasper Monument and the United Daughters of the Confederacy. This park is also the home of the beautiful Williams Music Pavilion which was established in 1907.

If you like Dynasty and all those juicy soap operas, visit the High Battery and see its beautiful mansions. Most of these mansions were built by wealthy landlords and shipping merchants. You could find a few historic houses in this area, including the Edmondston- Alston House. This house was built in 1920 and it used to be the mansion of a Scottish shipping magnate named Charles Edmondston. This house has three storeys and it has the scenic view of the Charleston Harbor.

The Battery is a contradiction. This scenic place was once a military base. But, despite of its bloody civil war past, there's something about this place that exudes romance, peace, and serenity.

The Rainbow Row

The Rainbow Row is definitely one of the most beautiful neighborhoods in the city, it's located just along the Battery. It is the home of the thirteen pastel-colored colonial houses. It is the most photographed tourist attraction in the Charleston. This neighborhood is often the reason why Chucktown became the ultimate destination for photographers and Instagrammers.

The Rainbow Row

The Rainbow Row is located on East Bay Street. This neighborhood has a rich history. Before the civil war, the merchants constructed commercial buildings. The ground floor of these buildings was used as a store while the second floor was used as the living quarters of the businessmen, their family, and slaves.

After the civil war, this neighborhood was destroyed. It almost looked like a slum. But, in the 1920s, a woman named Susan Frost bought six buildings, but she has no money to restore the buildings to its original form. In 1931, Dorothy Ledge (the wife of the Associate Justice Lionel Ledge) bought a section of the neighborhood (99 to 101 East Bay). She always loves the colonial Caribbean colors and so, she painted the houses pink. The neighbors liked what Dorothy did and so they eventually followed suit.

There are a lot of myths that attempt to explain the rainbow color scheme of the houses. According to one legend, the houses were painted in different colors so drunk sailors can remember which house they were staying. According to another tale, the merchants painted the stores different colors so the illiterate slaves can tell which building to shop just by looking at the color.

The Rainbow Row

This neighborhood is not only hauntingly beautiful. It makes you feel like you're in the colonial times. It's stunning, whimsical, and definitely picture-perfect.

St. Michael's Church and Graveyard

The St. Michael's Church is one of the oldest and most prominent buildings in Charleston. It was built in 1751 and it used to be affiliated with the Church of England. But, after the American Revolution, it became an Episcopal church. It is now the church of the diocese of South Carolina.

St. Michael's Church

The church has a mix of Gothic Revival, Victorian, and Colonial architecture. It has a tall pointed tower, making it one of the tallest buildings in Charleston for a very long time.

The church has a majestic white exterior and a grand Victorian-style altar. You could also find a grand chandelier in the middle of the church.

St. Michael's Church is located in 71 Broad St., Charleston. It's open from 9 am to 4 pm from Monday to Thursday. The church is open only up to 12 noon every Saturday and Sunday.

The Old Exchange and Provost Dungeon

The Old Exchange is one of the most important landmarks in Charleston. It was built in 1771 as a custom house. This Georgian building is one of the most beautiful architectural gems in the city. But, like most beautiful places, it has a dark past. It's haunted with tortured souls as it was once used as a prison during the American Revolution. The building houses the Provost Dungeon where prisoners were tortured, chained to the walls, and killed.

The Old Exchange

This building entertained leaders like George Washington. It was also one of the meeting places of the patriots where they discussed and debated the provisions of the United States Constitution. This historical building is also the site of many public slave auctions.

Today, The Old Exchange serves as a museum. It hosts a number of fun activities for kids, such as the pirate scavenger hunt, the George Washington scavenger hunt, and colonial Christmas tours. The Old Exchange is open from 9 am to 5 pm every day, but it's closed during holidays. Ticket costs $10 for adults and teens, $5 for children.

St. Phillips Church and Graveyard

St. Phillip's Church is a historic Episcopal church located at 142 Church Street, Charleston. It was built in 1836 on the site of a destroyed church that was established in 1680. It's located in the city's scenic French Quarter.

St. Phillip's Church

This church has a Greek revival architecture, but looks a bit like a Victorian building. It has a tall clock tower that you can see from almost anywhere in the city.

This towering building is one of the tallest buildings in Charleston. It is also a National Historic Landmark. This church has a rich history. A bishop named William Alexander Guerry was murdered in this church. It was also the site of the first state funeral. Its graveyard is the resting place of some of the Founding Fathers, pirate hunters, artists, politicians, and military generals.

Fort Sumter

Fort Sumter was built in 1811. It's special because it's where the civil war began. On April 12, 1861, the Confederate Soldiers opened fire and attacked the then Union-controlled fort.

Fort Sumter

Today, it's a popular tourist destination. A lot of travel companies offer tours around the area. Most of these tours include snacks. There's a lot to see in the area, including the Fort Summer National Monument, the Fort Sumter Visitor Education Center, and the Fort Moultrie. You could see cannons, flags, and fortifications.

This landmark is located off the coast of the Sullivan Island and it's open from 8:30 am to 5 pm.

Phone: +1 843-883-3123

Arthur Revenel Jr. Bridge

This bridge is one of the most beautiful cable-stayed bridges you'll ever see. It connects Charleston to a suburban town called Mount Pleasant.

It opened in 2005 and it was named after Congressman Arthur Ravenel – the person who raised funds for the construction of the bridge.

The Arthur Revenel Jr. Bridge looks like it's floating in the wind. It looks sleek, beautiful, and graceful. So, it's no wonder that it's one of the most photographed structures of the city.

Arthur Revenel Jr. Bridge

3

Unique Things to Do In Charleston

Charleston is a beach destination, a historical mecca, and a culinary paradise. Everything in this city is interesting and easy on the eyes. It gives you a unique experience that you will forever cherish. Below is the list of the most unique things that you can do in this city.

See the Beautiful and Historical Antebellum Houses

Charleston is a cultural melting pot. It's filled with immigrants from Spain, England, Scotland, Germany, Ireland, and France. So, it's no surprise that you'll see a number of colorful French, Victorian, Georgian, and Spanish houses around the city.

One of the best and cheapest things to do in Charleston is to check out the city's stunning and historic houses. Aside from the houses in the Rainbow Row, here's a list of beautiful homes that you should see in the holy city:

· **Joseph Manigault House**

This historic house is located just across the Charleston Museum. It's a national historic landmark and was designed by Gabriel Manigault, a known American architect and Joseph's brother. This house is located at the corner of John and Meeting streets. It was built in 1803.

The house is well-preserved, so it looked a lot like it did decades ago. Everything in the house exudes class and opulence. It has a wooden spiral staircase that's interesting and captivating. The rooms are decorated with chandeliers, beautiful paintings, and beautiful furniture. This is not really surprising because Joseph Manigault is one of the wealthiest people in South Carolina. He had a number of rice plantations and he has more than two hundred slaves.

This house used to be a status symbol, but it's is now part of the Charleston Museum.

· The Aiken-Rhett House

This house is located at 48 Elizabeth Street. It was built in 1820 by a wealthy Charleston merchant named John Robinson. His ships transported rice and other crops. Unfortunately, the French burned his cargo ships and so he sold his house to William Aiken in 1827.

William Aiken used this house as a rental home until his death. His son, William Aiken Jr., inherited this house. William Jr. later on became a famous politician and the governor of South Carolina. The house was renovated and it became the home of the younger Aiken's impressive art collection.

This yellow house remained in the Aiken family until 1975 when they decided to donate it to Charleston Museum. This house gives you a sneak peek of the antebellum life – the period of slavery and agriculture before the civil war.

This house/museum is open daily from 10 am to 5 pm. The entrance fee costs $12 for adults and $5 for kids. Kids under 6 years old can visit this house for free.

· The Calhoun Mansion

The Calhoun Mansion is located at 16 Meeting Street. This historic house is a symbol of opulence, power, and wealth. It was built in 1876 for George Williams. But, when he died, his son in law named Patrick Calhoun inherited this house. Calhoun was one of the most powerful "railroad baron" at that time.

This house is huge and it has more than thirty rooms. It appeared in various TV shows and movies, including "Gunfight at Branson Creek" and "North and South".

· The Edmondston- Alston House

This historic Regency-style home is located at 21 East Battery Street. It was built in 1820 for a rich shipping merchant named Charles Edmondston. In 1838, a wealthy Lowcountry rice producer named Charles Alston bought this house. It stayed within the Alston family for years until Union General Rufus Saxton occupied this house during the Civil War.

This house was turned into a museum in 1973 to preserve its beautiful façade and architectural integrity.

· William Gibbes House

This Georgian mansion is located at 64 South Battery in Charleston. It is one of the National Historic Landmarks in the United States. It was built in 1689 for William Gibbes. This beautiful old house is one of the most expensive real estate properties in the city.

· Pink House

The Pink House is one of the most photographed houses in Charleston. It's located at 17 Chalmers Street. It is the second oldest surviving residential building in the city, next to the Rhett House.

This house is made of pinkish Bermuda stone and it was built in 1694 (although the date is the subject of a dispute). This house used to be a tavern and it's owned by several people over the years, including James Gordon, artist Alice Huger Smith, and Victor Morawetz. This beautiful house also used to be the home of Madame Mincey.

The Pink House is now used as an art gallery. And, guess what? The property is for sale.

· Miles Brewton House

This historic Georgian building is located at 27 King Street. It has managed to stay within the Brewton family since 1769. This house was inherited by Rebecca Brewton Motte and it's where the British officer Henry Clinton stayed during the American Revolution. Today, the house is owned by a Brewton descendant Lee Manigault.

This house has an impressive gate, twelve Corinthian columns, and a ravishing balcony.

This elegant house is hauntingly beautiful. The wooden staircase is captivating. It has a sophisticated living room that makes you feel like you're in a Victorian mansion.

Shop at the City Market

The City Market was built in 1739, making it one of the oldest market complexes in the United States. Its market hall has a rustic Greek Revival architecture. This hall is also the home of the Confederate Museum.

The Charleston City Market is probably one of the most vibrant market-places you'll ever see in your lifetime. It has over one hundred vendors selling all kinds of things – spices, silverware, jewelry, paintings, crafts, and clothing. You could also find the famous Charleston sweetgrass baskets. You could also find a lot of shops in the area, including Caviar & Bananas, Jolin's, Charleston Hat Shop, The Fishin' Duck Inc., WonderWorks, Gita's Gourmet, and Passing Fancy.

This market is located at 188 Meeting Street. It's open daily from 9:30 to 6 pm (but, the market closes at 10 pm every Friday and Saturday).

Explore Charleston's Other Beach Towns

Charleston is known for its historical streets and colorful houses. But, it's also a popular beach destination. There are five beach towns that are less than an hour away from the heart of the holy city. No wonder that it's a haven for surfers and beach bums.

If you're tired of walking around the city, head to the best Charleston destination listed below.

Folly Island

Folly Island is also known as the "edge of America". This charming beach town is just approximately 15 minutes away from the downtown area. It has powdered sand and it's a good place for activities like kayaking, sailing, and surfing. It's a paradise for wave seekers.

There's a lot to see on this island, you can stroll along the bay walk leading to the island's surf tower. You can eat in a beachfront restaurant. You can even shop at the island's business district. You can also witness the beautiful Folly sunset.

Kiawah Island

Kiawah Island has a ten kilometer unspoiled white sand coastline. It also has maritime forests and white sand dunes. This paradise also has a fair share of wild animals, such as sea turtles, alligators, bobcats, whitetail deer, and majestic seabirds.

This island is great for fishing and sightseeing. It also has a golf course and a tennis court. Kiawah Island is a green paradise. It has fields that look like emerald gems from afar. This island is a gated resort community and it's private, so you would have to pay a gate fee which costs $15.

Unfortunately, it's difficult to get to the island via bus if you're not staying in a resort. The best way to get to this island is drive a car via Interstate 95. You can also take a taxi, but it could cost you $80 (for one way trip).

Sullivan's Island

This island has a small town vibe. It's warm, homey, and beautiful. It has a rich history, too. The island was a site of a major battle on June 28, 1776, during the American Revolution.

There are a lot of things to see in Sullivan's Island. You can do kite surfing. You can also see the island lighthouse. You could also visit Fort Moultry, a historic place where Edgar Allan Poe used to live (from 1827 to 1828).

Sullivan's Island is picture perfect. It exudes serenity, peace, beauty, and even, patriotism. It's a good place to relax and just enjoy the cold breeze.

Seabrook Island

Seabrook Island is about 40 minutes away from downtown Charleston. It's located right next to Kiawah Island. You can walk around the beach or go fishing. You can go horseback riding or paddle boarding. You can also ride on a pirate ship!

This scenic beach town is a good place to relax, meditate, and think about the good things of life.

Isle of Palms

Isle of Palms is a beach town about 33 minutes away from downtown Charleston. This beach has a long pier. This town is the home of many resorts, oceanfront hotels, and inns.

There are a lot of things that you can do in the Isle of Palms. You can go on a Barrier Island Eco Tour. You go dolphin-watching or fishing. It also has a golf course named Wild Dunes.

Shop at King Street

King Street is located at the heart of Charleston's French Quarter district.

This street is lined with beautiful buildings and palmettos. It's so beautiful that you'd actually think for a second that you're in Paris. It is posh and it's the hub of artists, culinary masters, creative, and musician.

This street is the home of various art galleries, including the Hagan Fine Art. It's also the home of restaurants and unique stores, such as:

- **<u>Blue Bicycle Books</u>**

This bookstore is a paradise for book lovers. This shop sells "hard to find" books and also signed copies famous artists' work, such as Margaret Mitchell, Harper Lee, and William Faulkner.

- **George C. Birlant & Co.**

This antique store was founded in 1922, making it one of the oldest antique stores in the South. This store also produces and sells the classic Charleston Battery Bench.

- **Worthwhile**

This is a quaint gift shop that sells a wide variety of goods, including candles, soaps, books, shoes, and necklaces.

- **Croghan's Jewel Box**

This jewelry store is one hundred years old. It has a quaint façade and an elegant interior. The jewels are displayed in glass covered tables. You can also find expensive chandeliers hang from the ceiling. This store sells extremely expensive jewelry, including Princess Diana's ring.

This street is also the home of other amazing stores, such as Sugar Snap Pea, Finicky Filly, Berlin's, Alex and Ani, Anthropologie, Loft, Banana Republic, Bebe, Brooks Brothers, Gap, H & M, and Forever 21.

Explore The City's Iconic Streets

One of the best things about Charleston is that you don't have to spend a lot of money to enjoy its beauty. You can simply stroll around the downtown area and explore the following historic and scenic streets:

- **Broad Street**

This street is one of the most beautiful streets in the city. It's the home of St. Michael's Church and the Gallery Row. This is definitely a paradise for art lovers.

- **The Chalmers Street**

This street has Cobblestone pathways. It is the home of the Old Slave Mart Museum. If you want to discover the hardships of African Americans, you should head to this street.

- **Church Street**

This street is the home of the glorious St. Philip's Episcopal Church. You could also find the Dock Street Theatre (America's first playhouse).

- **East Bay Street**

The East Bay Street is located in the Battery. It is the home of beautiful antebellum buildings. You could also find a number of restaurants in the area, including High Cotton and Poogan's Smokehouse.

- **Tradd Street**

This street exudes nothing but southern charm. This street has colorful buildings, secret gardens, and exquisite metal carriage lanterns.

- **Legare Street**

This street looks like a wonderland. It is the home to exquisite gardens. It is also the home of the Sword Gate House – one of the most beautiful houses in Charleston.

- **Queen Street**

This is a paradise for foodies. It is the home of the most popular Lowcountry restaurants, including Husk, S2 Queen, and Poogan's Porch.

Magnolia Plantation and Gardens

This Magnolia Plantation is one of the most beautiful places in the city. It was established in the 1676 by the wealthy Drayton family before the American Revolution.

This plantation looks like a paradise. Everything about this place exudes romance. You could walk on paths lined with colorful Azaleas. You can also explore the Plantation House. You could also cruise on a rice field. You could also explore the beautiful Audubon Swamp Garden. You can even learn about the pain of the African American slaves. You can visit the Magnolia Cabin Project, a collection of slave houses.

There's a lot to see in this plantation. There's also a restaurant, café, and a gift shop. It also has a zoo. You can even rent this plantation for private events and weddings.

See the 500 Year Old Angel Oak

The Angel Oak is a 500 year old tree located in the Angel Oak Park on Johns Island in Charleston, South Carolina. It is one of the oldest trees in the United States.

This oak tree is huge. Its branches extend out like they have a life of their own. There's something about this tree that's so majestic. The branches look like they are crawling out the trunk. This tree is absolutely marvelous!

After checking out the Angel Oak, you can also do horseback riding at the James Island County Park, you could visit a brewery called Low Tide Brewing, and lastly, you can do Whale Watching.

Explore the Middleton Place

The Middleton Place is one of the oldest and most beautiful landscaped gardens in the United States. It is located at 4300 Ashley River Road, Dorchester Country. It's just a fifteen minute drive from downtown

Charleston.

This garden is definitely one of the most beautiful places you'll ever see in your lifetime. It has picturesque landscapes. It was established in 1730 by an agricultural tycoon named John Williams.

The whole place is hauntingly beautiful. It is the home of many statues, colorful flowers, and oak trees with dripping Spanish moss.

You could see ducks and even alligators swimming in the creek. It almost feels like it's the Garden of Eden.

This plantation open daily from 9 am to 5 pm. The entrance fee costs $49.

Do Yoga at a Local Brewery

Yoga is one of the best exercises. It's good for your health, it keeps you fit, and it clarified your mind.

Yoga can do wonders to your health. It decreases your blood pressure and it improves the quality of your sleep. It improves your flexibility and posture. But, if you want to take your yoga practice to the next level, do it in a brewery. Who knew that beer and yoga can be a good mix?

Many breweries in Charleston like Ghost Monkey, Frothy Beard, and the Holy City Brewery offer yoga classes. A one hour yoga class costs about $15 to $20 and it comes with a pint of cold beer, too!

Holy City Brewery
+1 843-225-5623
4155 Dorchester Rd, Charleston

4

Best Museums in Charleston

Charleston has a rich history. It was once the home of the Native Americans. It was also once a slave state where wealthy merchants built their empires with the help of their slaves. It even played a huge role in the civil war. So, it's no surprise that it's the home of many grand museums. It even has a street filled with museums aptly called the "museum mile". Below are the best museums that you should visit.

Charleston Museum

The Charleston Museum was founded in 1773, making it one of the oldest museums in the United States. But, the present modern museum building was built in 1980.

This museum has an impressive collection of artworks, weapons, Egyptian artifacts, items from the American Revolution, and the tools used by the original settlers in Charleston – the Native Americans. This museum also houses a number of fossils, specimens, and mounted skeletons of the world's largest flying bird, the Pelagornis.

The Charleston Museum also owns two historical houses – the Joseph Manigault House and the Heyward- Washington House.

This interesting museum is located at 360 Meeting St. and it's open from every day from 9 am to 5 pm (it's open from 12 pm to 5 pm every Sunday). Admission ticket costs $18 (which includes entry to the Heyward- Washington House and the Joseph Manigault House).

Gibbes Museum of Art

The Gibbes Museum of Art is located at 135 Meeting St. It has a solid and fascinating Greek Revival architecture designed by one of the most prolific architects in the United States- Frank Pierce Milburn. This building was built in 1905. It was named after its benefactor James Schoolbred Gibbes.

The Gibbes Museum of Art has a collection of over ten thousand fine arts. It is truly a paradise for art enthusiasts. It showcases the artworks of American artists, such as Jane Peterson, Mabel Dwight, Martha Walter, Horace Talmage, Grace Albee, William McCullough, Louise Nevelson, and Chakaia Booker.

This elegant museum does more than display exquisite artwork. It also holds art classes. It also has a lecture hall, a cafeteria, and a souvenir store.

Nathaniel Russell House

The Nathaniel Russell House is a historic home transformed into a museum. This neoclassical home is one of the most important colonial houses. It is one of the National Historic Landmarks in the United States.

This house is made of reddish bricks and it has an exquisite spiral staircase and an elegant interior. Being in this mansion makes you feel like you're part of a wealthy antebellum clan. The halls are majestic and the dining hall is a bit intriguing. You could even see a harp.

This house was built for Nathaniel Russell, a wealthy shipping tycoon in 1765. It was a symbol of wealth and power. The house was later sold to a wealthy rice farmer Robert Allston. It was later sold to a group of nuns. And so, it became a boarding school from 1870 to 1905. It was subsequently bought by two wealthy families. In 1955, the Historic Charleston Foundation purchased this house and transformed it into a museum.

This splendid home is located at 51 Meeting Street. It is open daily from 10 am to 5 am. Tickets cost $12 (for adults) and $5 (for kids 6 to 16). Kids under five years old can see this museum for free.

Confederate Museum

The Confederate Museum has an interesting Greek revival architecture. It was located at 188 Meeting St. in the city's downtown area. An organization called Daughters of Confederacy owns this building.

This museum showcases memorabilia of the Confederate States of America (1861 to 1865). In case you don't know, the CSA was established during the Montgomery Convention and it was initially formed by 7 slave states – Alabama, Mississippi, Florida, Louisiana, Georgia, Texas, and South Carolina. Later on, Virginia, Arkansas, North Carolina, Tennessee, Missouri, and Kentucky joined the seven states to form a new "country".

This museum stores the flags, military uniforms, and weapons of the Confederate era. It is open from 11 am to 3:30 pm. Entrance fee costs $5 for adults and $3 for children.

Karpeles Manuscript Museum

This is a paradise for aspiring writers and those who like to read. This museum has the largest collection of original manuscripts in the world. It was founded in 1983 by David and Marsha Karpeles, wealthy real estate developers from California.

This museum has a Greek Revival architecture and it used to be a Methodist church. This museum contains the original manuscripts and documents used to produce the Roget's Thesaurus, the Webster's Dictionary, Darwin's Theory of Evolution, and the Bill of Rights.

This museum is located at the 68 Spring St. and it's open from 11 am to 4 pm. It's open from Tuesday to Sunday.

5

Art Therapy: The Best Art Galleries in Downtown Charleston

Charleston's French Quarter is one of the most famous neighborhoods in the city. It is the home of colorful and stunning buildings like the Pink House Tavern and the Old Slave Mart. But, it is also the home of around 40 art galleries. Some of these galleries are so elegant and post that they serve snacks and wine. Below are the best galleries that you shouldn't miss.

Hagan Fine Art

Hagan Fine Art is one of the most elegant art galleries in Charleston. It was established in 2010 by a well-known artist named Karen Hewitt Hagan. This gallery is located at 177 King Street in the beautiful French Quarter. It's the home of beautiful landscape paintings of artists like Gloria Mani, Sara Jane Doberstein, Amy Dixon, Olessia Maximenko, and Karen Hewitt Hagan. The gallery also showcases a number of wildlife sculptures and they sell custom chandeliers, too. You can also rent the gallery as an event venue.

Courtyard Gallery

Courtyard Art Gallery was established in 1984 and it's located at 149 ½ East Bay Street. It's just a few steps away from the Rainbow Row and the Market. This gallery showcases different artworks of a few South Carolinian artisans – paper sculpture, jewelry, photography, stained glasses, and more. It's a paradise for art enthusiasts and collectors.

Gordon Wheeler Gallery

Gordon Wheeler Gallery was established in 1990. It is located at 180 East Bay Street and it showcases Gordon's surreal and captivating paintings. When you look at his work, feels like each brush stroke tells a story.

This gallery is hard to miss - it has a beautiful façade with red sunshades that says "180 Gordon Wheeler Gallery".

LePrince Fine Art

This gallery is located at 184 King Street, at the heart of Charleston's French Quarter. This posh space showcases the impressionist paintings of its founder, Kevin LePrince, and other up and coming artists, including Mark Bailey, Angie Renfro, and Vicki Robinson.

The gallery exudes elegance and class. The white walls are filled with magnificent paintings and you can find a delicate chandelier hanging from the ceiling. It occasionally hosts art lessons and you can rent it for events.

Low Country Artists Gallery

This gallery was founded in 1982, making it the oldest artist-own gallery in the city. It is located at 148 East Bay St. and it showcases the works of its owners – Stephanie Hamlet, Monnie Johnson, Ivo Kerseemakers, Rana Jordahl, Sandra Roper, and Norma Cable. The paintings depict local scenes and landscapes. These artworks are so beautiful that they invoke euphoria and bliss.

6

Luxury without Breaking the Bank: The Best Hotels in Charleston

Charleston may be the number one city in the world. But, it's not as expensive as Paris or Sydney. You'd be surprised to know that the city has a number of elegant and yet, budget-friendly hotels.

Comfort Inn Downtown Charleston

This three star hotel is clean, organized, and cozy. It has an outdoor rooftop pool and a gym. It also offers laundry, photocopying, and fax services.

Comfort Inn lives up to its name as it provides comfort to its guests at a reasonable price. Room rates can go as low as $99 per night. It's located at 144 Bee Street, just a few minutes away from the historic streets of Charleston.

Phone:+1 843-577-2224

Town and Country Inn

Town and Country Inn is a three star hotel located at 2008 Savannah Highway, West of the Ashley, Charleston. It exudes elegance, and it has friendly staff, too. The rooms are clean and exquisite. It's perfect for honeymooners and those who prioritize comfort.

This hotel has a stylish dining area, a laundry area, and a gym. The rooms also have a refrigerator and a microwave oven. And best of all, these rooms cost at least $99.

Phone:+1 843-571-1000

Holiday Inn Express

This three-star hotel is located at 250 Spring Street, Charleston, just a few steps away from the historic center of Charleston.

Holiday Inn Express has a warm vibe and homey vibe. It has an outdoor pool and a fitness center. The rooms are clean and have great views. They are also pet-friendly and comes with a coffee machine, a work desk, a flat screen TV, and an immaculate bathroom. These rooms cost as low as $126.

Phone:+1 843-722-4000

Barksdale House Inn

Barksdale House Inn is comfortably nestled in the city's historic center. This house was built in 1778 and it has a strong European vibe. This yellow house is one of the most popular bed and breakfast in the city.

This inn makes you feel like you're in an old mansion. It has classy furniture and some rooms have four poster beds. Everything about this three star hotel makes you feel like a royalty.

The Barksdale House Inn is located at 27 George Street. It is just a few minutes away from the Old City Market and a fifteen minute walk away from the South Carolina Aquarium. This place is not only stunning, it's affordable, too. Rooms cost at least $159.

Phone:+1 843-577-4800

Hilton Garden Inn

Hilton Garden Inn is a castle-looking hotel located at 45 Lockwood

Drive. It has a rooftop pool and friendly staff.

This four star hotel is not only beautiful; it also has a great location. It's just minutes away from the city's most popular neighborhood and landmarks. It's also surprisingly affordable. Rooms cost at least $183.

Phone:+1 843-637-4074

7

A Culinary Paradise: The Best Restaurants and Cafes in Charleston

Mondello,Charleston

Charleston is known as South Carolina's culinary paradise. It is the ultimate food destination. So, it's no surprise that you'll find a number of great restaurants around the city. When you're in Charleston, don't forget to try its delicious delicacies, such as rock shrimp salad, duck fat fries, grilled oysters, lobster roll, crab toast, fried mac & cheese, barbecue shrimp, and turkey panini.

Whether you're into fine dining or street food, there's something in Charleston that's right for your taste and budget.

Be Prepared for a Culinary Adventure: Top Restaurants in the Holy City

Charleston is, no doubt, one of the hottest food destinations in the United States. It's the home of many traditional Southern restaurants. But, you can find also find European and Asians restaurants all over the city. Below is the list of the best restaurants in the holy city.

Husk

Husk is a restaurant housed in an elegant restored Victorian building. This restaurant makes you feel like you're in a different time. It's a good place for dates and celebrations. This restaurant has a great ambience. Everything about it screams luxury. But, what makes this restaurant special is its delectable Lowcountry dishes.

Sean Brock, an award-winning chef, runs this restaurant, making sure that the menu items are not only delicious, but also innovative and unique. You could try fire roasted oysters with South Carolina honey. You can also try the restaurant's griddled shrimp with red eye gravy. They also serve dishes like cornmeal fried catfish, confit duck leg, and cider glazed chicken with honey glazed apple.

Husk is sophisticated, fancy, and surprisingly, affordable, too. What more could you ask for?

Address: 76 Queen St, Charleston
  Phone: +1 843-577-2500

Fig

Fig was founded in 2003 by Adam Nemirow and Mark Late - people who are genuinely passionate about creating tasty and exquisite dishes. This restaurant uses local ingredients. This means that they empower local farmers and hog raisers. They serve unique dishes like Burnt Eggplant and Cottage Cheese. They also serve Beef Tartare, Brasstown Ribeye, and Ricotta Gnocchi Ala Bolognese. Its award winning chef, Jason Stanhope, uses French cooking techniques in preparing the restaurant's southern dishes.

Fig has interesting cocktails, too. These cocktails are not only beautiful, colorful, and photogenic. They also have exquisite and unique ingredients, such as valvet falernum, hibiscus, cardamaro, bourbon, elderflower, braulio, and black salt.

The restaurant is open from 5:30 pm to 10:00 pm. It's located at 232 Meeting St., Charleston.

Phone: +1 843-805-5900

Evo Pizzeria

Evo Pizzeria is located at 1075 East Montague Avenue, North Charleston, South Carolina. This restaurant has a simple red brick exterior and a homey ambience. But, what makes this restaurant special is its wood-fired pizza.

This pizzeria is open from Monday to Saturday from 11 am to 10 pm. They serve unique salads and pies. They also offer "out of this world" pizzas like pumpkin and chorizo pizza. This place definitely serves the best pizza in the city.

82 Queen

82 Queen is located at, you guessed it right – 82 Queen Street, right at the heart of the city's French Quarter. This high end restaurant was founded in 1982 by Chef Steve Kish, Joe Sliker, and Harvey Poole.

This restaurant exudes class and Southern hospitality. 82 Queen serves an award winning crab soup. They also serve barbeque shrimps, chicken salad wrap, fried oyster mac and cheese, jambalaya, short ribs, and Caesar salad.

This restaurant is amazing and affordable, too. Meals usually cost $15 to $35.

Minero

This restaurant makes you feel like you are in Mexico. It has an exquisite bar and diner-style couches. You could see medieval-like chandeliers hanging from the ceiling. This classy restaurant is located at East Bay St., Charleston, South Carolina. They're open from 11 am to 10 pm.

Minero is perfect for after-work drinks. They save Mexican dishes like fried catfish tacos, roasted shrimp tacos, guacamole and chips, queso ranchero, and chopped salad. Minero also has an impressive list of thirst-quenching and mind-shaking cocktails.

Poogan's Porch

Poogan's Porch is located at 72 Queen Street. It uses traditional Southern cooking techniques. It was established in 1978. This place is so popular that it's frequented by politicians, celebrities, picky tourists, and locals.

This restaurant serves crab soup, mac & cheese, fried chicken salad, crab cake, wedge salad, and Lowcountry omelet. This place is affordable, too. Meals cost $15 to $30.

Of Laughter and Coffee: The Best Cafes in the City

Charleston is known as a culinary paradise. It's a good place to eat oysters and authentic Southern dishes. But, this is city is a haven for coffee drinkers, too. Below is the list of the best cafes and coffee shops in the city.

The Orange Spot Coffee House

The Orange Spot Coffee House is located at 1011 East Montague Avenue. It opens at 6 am and closes at 6 pm. It serves rich coffee and a few snacks, including coffee cake, blueberry muffin, savory scone, quiche, and grilled cheese.

Gaulart & Maliclet Fast and French Inc

This café transports you to France. It has a strong Parisian ambience, so it's a good place to hang out and read a good book. They serve delicious French-pressed coffee and European snacks, such as Turkey and goat cheese sandwich, Smoked salmon sandwich, croissant, grand petite dejeuner, half vegetarian croq baguette ham, and chickens du jour. This café also serve sparkling water from France.

This café is open from Monday to Saturday (8 am to 4 pm every Monday to Wednesday, 8 am to 10 pm Thursday to Saturday).

Address: 98 Broad St, Charleston

Mercantile and Mash

Mercantile and Mash is one of the hippest and most modern hangout area in the city. The drinks are all created by a renowned coffee master named Michael Mai.

This coffee shop is located at 701 East Bay Street, amidst the historical buildings. It is open daily (7 am to 7 pm Monday to Friday, Saturday 8 am to 3 pm, Friday 8 am to 3 pm).

City Lights Coffee

This quaint café is a hideout for many artists and writers. It has free wifi so you can find a lot of freelancers and digital nomads hanging out in this area. There's something about this coffee shop that instantly makes you feel at home.

The City Lights Coffee Shop is located at 141 Market Street. It is open daily (7 am to 8 pm Monday to Thursday; 7 am to 9 pm Friday; 8 am to 6 pm Sunday and Saturday).

The Rise Coffee Bar

The Rise is known for its citrus cold brew. It's located on the ground floor of the Restoration Hotel.

This coffee shop serves coffee from exotic parts of the world, including Guatemala, Kenya, El Salvador, and Brazil. It is open from 7 am to 5 pm during weekdays and from 8 am to 5 pm during weekends.

8

The Best Bars and Night Clubs in Charleston

Charleston is laid back during the day and quite electric at night. It's a great place to just relax, drink a good wine, and have a good time. This city is oozing with positive vibes, bright lights, hypnotizing music, and intoxicating cocktails.

Bars and Pubs

The city is a paradise for craft beer enthusiasts. It has more than ten breweries. So, it's no surprise that you'll find a number of awesome pubs and bars in the city.

Tin Roof

Tin Roof is located at 1117 Magnolia Road. This pub has a strong Southern vibe. It plays country music and serves snacks, sandwiches, fries, breakfast wraps, and hot dogs. They also serve delicious draft, domestic, and house beers.

Voodoo Tiki Bar

This bar is located at 15 Magnolia Drive. The Voodoo Tiki Bar has an eerie and yet, classy vibe. It's like you're lured into a world of witchcraft.

The Voodoo Tiki Bar serves Baja Shrimp and Bacon Cheeseburger. Happy Hour starts 4 pm and ends at 7 pm from Monday to Friday.

Edmund's Oast

This is actually a restaurant and it's located at 108 1 Morrison Drive. But, the Edmund's Oast has a wide selection of cocktails, beers, and wines. In fact, it has its own brewery.

This restaurant was named after an English brewer who moved to Charleston in 1760s. He had donated a lot of money during the American Revolution. This is the reason why he was called the "Rebel Brewer".

Faculty Lounge

Faculty Lounge is a hip bar with interesting furniture and light pieces. It used to be a neighborhood bar frequented by teachers, hence, the name. This bar is located at 391 Huger Street. This bar has an in house DJ and occasionally hosts Beyonce nights. But, the best thing about this bar is that it has a great selection of interesting and original cocktails.

The Faculty Lounge is located at 391 Huger St.

Moe's Crosstown Tavern

This pub-style restaurant has a hip vibe. It serves burgers, mozzarella sticks, chicken tenders, and jalapeno poppers. It also has a wide tap beer collection.

This tavern is located on Rutledge Avenue. It opens at 11 am and closes at 2 am.

Most Electric Night Clubs

Charleston is a city of beautiful people, Southern warmth, and picturesque neighborhoods. But, it has a vibrant nightlife, too. Below is the list of the best bars in the city.

Mynt

This is a popular college bar located at 135 Calhoun Street. Mynt is filled with beautiful people and mind-blowing music. This nightclub has a fascinating youthful energy. This club has a wild and spunky vibe and it also has an impressive menu and an impressive wine list. The bartenders are friendly and they sometimes offer free rounds for birthday celebrants.

The Commodore

If you don't like techno music, head to the Commodore. This is located at 504 Meeting Street. It's an old school jazz club where you could drink cold beer and dance to some cool music.

The Commodore has an exquisite bar dripped with elegant chandeliers. This bar serves original cocktails, domestic, craft, and imported beers.

There's something about this club that's both relaxing and fun. It has a classy interior with chandeliers, broken mirror liquor display, and leather Chester-style couches. But, it also has a youthful energy that's both captivating and contagious.

King Street Public House

The King Street Public House is one of the leading nightspots in the city. It's located at 549 Upper King Street.

This club has everything you could possibly ask for – beautiful crowd, great music, colorful lights, and mind-blowing drinks. It's also located at the heart of the city's French Quarter. It's a good place to meet new people, dance, and just have a good time.

Silver Dollar

Silver Dollar has a small town club vibe. It has a simple exterior and the whole place is not covered with laser-like lights. But, this is where well-known hip hop artists perform.

The Silver Dollar is located at 478 King Street. It's open daily from 7 pm to 2 am.

Trio

Trio is the premier bachelor and bachelorette party site in Charleston. It's a good place to chill, drink delicious cocktails, and meet beautiful people. This club has VIP suites, too.

Trio is usually used for private events, but it's open to the public from 10 pm to 2 am, Saturday and Sunday.

9

Everything You Need to Know Before Visiting Charleston

Charleston is one of the most beautiful cities in the United States. In fact, it was hailed as the best city in the world. But, below are the few things you need to know before you travel to the holy city.

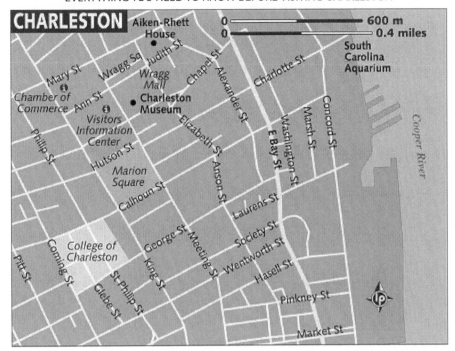

Weather

The Charleston could be a bit unpredictable. One day, it's hot and the next day, it's raining cats and dogs.

Springtime (March to May) is generally warm, but it rains at least five to six times a month. Summer days (June to August) are quite warm and comfortable. But, some days can get too hot.

Autumn days (September to November) can get cold and windy. It snows or rains at least seven days a month. Charleston is too cold during winter time (December to February). It rains or snows at least seven days a month.

Below are the average Charleston temperatures by month:

Month Average Temperature in Celsius

December 12 degrees

November 14 degrees

October 20 degrees

September 24 degrees

August 27.2 degrees

July 27.3 degrees

June 26 degrees

May 23 degrees

April 19 degrees

March 14 degrees

February 10 degrees

January 9 degrees

The Best Time to Visit the City

Charleston is most beautiful during the summer time. But, it could get too hot and this is also the tourism peak so some spots are crowded. The hotel rates and airfare are also expensive during this time.

If expensive lodging rates, skyrocketing fares, and crowds, do not bother you, visit Charleston during the summer time. But, if you're on a budget and you don't like hot weather, the best time to visit this city is November. The weather is cool and the lodging rates are extremely low. Plus, you get to really explore the city like a local.

How to Get Around the City

The best way to get around a city is through a car. So, if you're living in the United States or you have an international driving license, it's great to rent a car and invest in a good map. But, there are many other transportation options, too, including:

By Foot

Charleston is a walkable city. So, if you want to really enjoy the city and, at the same time, shed off the extra pounds, it's a good idea to walk around the city. You can stroll around by yourself or with your travel buddies. But, you can also join walking tours. Just make sure to wear comfortable shoes.

Pedi-cab

The city has a number of pedicabs (bicycle cab). Riding a pedicab is a bit "touristy", but it's a great way to enjoy the beauty of the city. You can find pedicabs on King Street and East Bay Street. These bicycle cabs run 24 hours a day and some of them are stationed in the Market. If you see a full cab, just call the driver and tell him that you want a ride. He'll ask a colleague to come and get you.

Taxi Cab

You can see taxi cab everywhere, but you can't flag them down. You have to call the taxi company ahead. The city has a number of taxi companies, including the Yellow Cab of Charleston, Black Cab, and Green Taxi.

Bike

A lot of hotels in Charleston have bicycles that guests can use. But, if your hotel does not offer this service, you can rent one in the Bicycle Shoppe located on Meeting Street. But, make sure to park your bicycles in the designated racks, otherwise the police would confiscate your bike.

Free Trolley

The CARTA (Charleston Area Regional Transport Authority) trolley is free. It's fully air-conditioned and it stops on the popular city landmarks. The drivers are friendly, but remember that this is not a "hop on, hop off" bus. The driver will not announce the next stop. So, grab the free map to get acquainted with the bus route. It's also helpful to tell the driver where you're headed.

Bus

There are a number bus companies operating Charleston. There are a number of bus stops, including the Rivers Avenue, Leeds Avenue, North Neck, King/Meeting Street, Savannah Highway, North Bridge, Coleman Boulevard, Mount Pleasant and Wando Circulator.

You can also book guided bus tours to save time and make the most out of your trip. Most 90 minute bus tours cost $23 per person.

Safety and Travel Tips

Charleston is, no doubt, one of the most beautiful cities you'll ever visit. The colorful Spanish and Georgian buildings will enchant you. Chucktown, as it's frequently called, is generally safe. But, even a city as beautiful as this one can be a little dangerous, too.

The downtown area is safer. But, it's good not to explore the city alone at night. Also, avoid North Charleston. It's a separate city next to Charleston (kind of like New York's Manhattan and Brooklyn). North Charleston has a high crime rate. Plus, you don't need to go there anyway as most tourist attractions are in downtown Charleston.

Beware of the fake police. A few criminals dress as policemen so they could do crimes such as rape, murders, and carjacking. If someone pulls you over, don't roll your window down unless you're sure that it's really the police.

Also, it's wise to check the weather before you visit Charleston. Hurricanes and storms are a bit common from July to November. Don't visit the city's beach towns when there's a storm or a forecasted hurricane.

Here's a list of few travel tips that you can use to make your Charleston vacation fun and hassle-free:

1. The best restaurants are listed earlier in this book. But, to truly enjoy your Charleston experience, you should try Charleston's unique dishes (and where you could find them), including:

- Duck club with duck fat fries (Tattooed Moose, 1137 Morrison Drive)
- Charred grilled oyster (Leon Oyster Shop, 698 King Street)
- Pumpkin Barbecue with pulled pork (The Rarebit, 474 King Street)
- Lobster roll (167 Raw, 289 East Bay)
- Big nasty (Hominy Grill, 207 Rutledge Avenue)
- Grilled cheese sandwich with nutella (Persimmon Café, 226 Calhoun Street)
- Five spice pork tacos (Bon Banh Mi, 162 Spring Street)
- Crab toast (The Ordinary, 544 King Street)

2.If you plan to see the gardens and plantations, visit this beautiful city during spring (March to April) when azaleas are in full bloom.

3.Floods are quite common in Charleston during the rainy season. So, make sure to wear sturdy boots and check the weather forecast frequently.

4.Walk around the city. This is the best way to explore the downtown area. If you're visiting during the summer time, feel free to wear flip flops.

5.You can join tours if you want to save time. But, it's also great to explore the city on your own.

6.You don't have to spend a lot of money to enjoy the beauty of

Charleston. You can just visit the historic streets and the Battery. You can also visit the city's stunning churches and parks.

7.If you like horror movies, join a ghost tour. You'll be surprised to know that there are a number of haunted houses in the holy city.

8.Charleston nightlife is great. But, you don't have to go to a nightclub if you don't want to. You can go see a comedy show instead. There's a number of comedy shows at Theatre 99 and The Black Fedora Comedy Mystery
   Theatre.

9.Get a free praline sample at several candy and dessert stores, including the Market Street Sweets (100 North Street), the Charleston Candy Kitchen (32 N Market Street), and the Charleston City Market (188 Meeting St).

10. If you're visiting Charleston during the Christmas season, drive to John's Island to see its colorful lights.

11. A lot of stores accept credit cards. But, make sure to carry cash.

12.People in Charleston are incredibly friendly. Don't hesitate to ask for directions if you're lost.

And don't forget bring a good camera. Charleston is a picture-perfect city and a good place to create awesome memories. Make sure that you capture the highlights of your Southern trip.

10

The Ultimate Charleston 3 Day Travel Itinerary

One of the best things about Charleston is that it's a compact city and most tourist spots are in one area. So, you can see a lot of spots in just three days. Below is the ultimate three day Charleston itinerary that you can use.

Day 1 – Museums and Historic Houses

Spend your first day touring the city's historic neighborhood. Here's a list of sites that you should visit:

1. The Museum Mile – This is a section of Meeting Street that's filled with museums, namely:

- The Aiken-Rhett House
- The Charleston Museum
- Joseph Manigault House
- The Children's Museum of the Lowcountry
- Confederate Museum
- Powder Magazine (the oldest public building in South Carolina)
- The Gibbes Museum of Art
- The Old Slave Mart Museum
- The South Carolina Historical Society
- Postal Museum
- Heyward-Washington House
- Nathaniel Russell House Museum

You don't have to visit all this museums. You can just choose the ones that captivate your interest.

2. The Old Exchange & Provost Dungeon

3. The Battery – You can see the Fort Sumter from the promenade, so you don't have to visit it unless you're really interested in learning more about the Civil War.

4. Walk around the famous neighborhoods in the city – including the French Quarter. Shop at King Street and check out its stunning art galleries, too.

5. See St. Phillips's and St. Michael's Church.

Day 2 – Shopping and Island Tours

Charleston is a shopping mecca and a beach destination. Here's a list of activities that you can do on the second day of your Charleston vacation:

1.Explore the city market.
2.Drive to John's Island and see the Angel Oak Tree.
3.Visit Sullivan and Kaiwah Island.
4.Watch the sunset at the Folly Beach.

Day 3 – Plantations and Gardens

Charleston is the home of agricultural resorts, gardens, and rice plantations. Here's a list of things you should do on your third day in the holy city:

1.Explore the Middleton Place

2.See the Magnolia Plantation and Gardens

If you're traveling with kids, it's also a good idea to the South Carolina Aquarium located in 100 Aquarium Wharf, Charleston.

Remember that this itinerary is just a guide. It's best to create your own itinerary, the one that fits your schedule and budget.

11

Conclusion

Thank you for reading this book!

I hope that this book was able to help you plan a fun and hassle-free Charleston vacation.

Here's a list of additional travel tips that you can use to make the most out of your Southern adventure:

- Charleston is a culinary mecca. So, eat as much local food as you can. Don't eat in KFC or McDonalds.
- If you're travelling during the summer time, don't forget to wear sunscreen. The Charleston sun is a bit brutal.
- Get travel insurance.
- Invest in a good camera so you can capture the beauty of the holy city.
- Write down the address of your hotel in case you get lost.
- Try the Charleston craft beer.
- Don't hesitate to smile at strangers. The locals are super friendly and accommodating.
- The parking fees are quite expensive, so park your car in a residential district so you don't have to pay anything. Then, just walk around the downtown area.
- Bill Murray lives in Charleston. If you want to see him, go to a Charleston Riverdogs game, he partly owns this baseball team.

And don't forget to have fun and take in all the beauty and picturesque views Charleston has to offer.

Thank you again for reading this book and good luck!

12

Thank You

I want to thank you for reading this book! I sincerely hope that you received value from it!

If you received value from this book, I want to ask you for a favour .Would you be kind enough to leave a review for this book on Amazon?